A
FEW
DAYS
IN
GENEVA

PHOTOGRAPHS BY
MARI MAHR

A
FEW
DAYS
IN
GENEVA

TRAVELLING LIGHT

Front cover photograph: from Virágom, Virágom

British Library CIP Data:
Mahr, Mari
A few days in Geneva: photographs. –
(Contemporary photography series).
1. Photography, Artistic
I. Title II. Series
779'.092'4 TR654
ISBN 0-906333-21-0 Hbk
ISBN 0-906333-23-7 Pbk

Contemporary Photography Series
A Few Days in Geneva: Photographs by Mari Mahr
First published in 1988 by Travelling Light
27 Sunbury Workshops, Swanfield Street, London E2
© 1988 Travelling Light
Foreword © 1988 Nigel Finch
Introduction © 1988 Tom Evans
Photographs © 1988 Mari Mahr
Layout by Colin Sackett, Coracle Press
Printed in Great Britain by The Whitefriars Press Ltd., Tonbridge, Kent.

CONTENTS

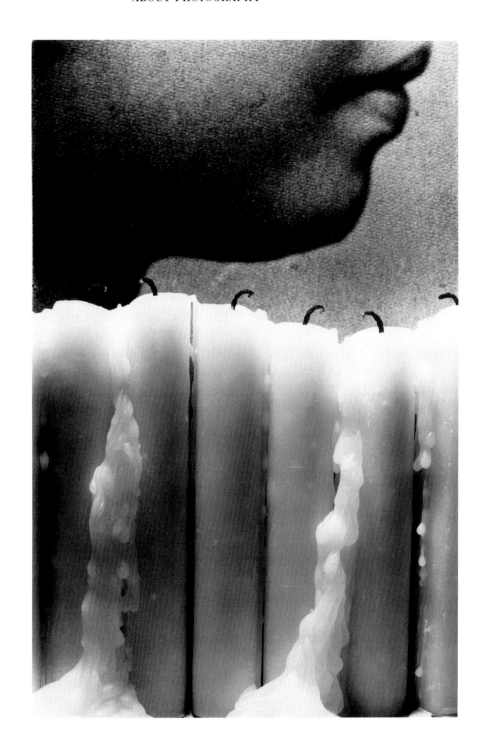

It's not easy writing about somebody you know well. Worse when they wouldn't thank you for a eulogy or pompous puff. But if these photographs are a first encounter with Mari Mahr, I should warn you, there is more to them than meets the eye . . .

It must be fifteen years since Mari moved into the vacant flat above mine. As somebody newly arrived in Britain, Mari had few possessions and I watched intrigued to see how from the grab bag of objects brought from her native Hungary she not only staked a claim to her patch but established a Hungarian toehold in suburban London.

Strings of red paprikas appeared in our shared kitchen and Hungarian sausages sat coiled in the larder. Curious religious icons, Catholic badges of arms and legs, votives for healing, were hung on the walls. Always discrete, these strange little fragments, touchstones of an exotic eastern European connection, started to impose themselves on the atmosphere of the house.

Then it started to happen, things disappeared, objects were moved. At first I hardly noticed but when a wall-hanging disappeared, reappeared and a pot plant had vanished instead I knew something was up.

They always came back in one piece but ask any questions of where or why and Mari's response was always, 'Later', or 'You'll see'.

The invitation to 'see' finally arrived. Upstairs in her bedroom, which doubled as a studio, the objects had acquired a new life. Strange stories, situations, memories were conjured in a sequence of photographs spread around the room. Although they were all of the Putney house in which we lived they seemed to deny the suburban reality I knew, inventing a new world. And whilst I clearly recognised the objects from my room they had, in the photos, acquired a new purpose.

Just as I had tried to piece together something of Mari's history from those fragmentary souvenirs of her past so she seemed to be fabricating a world from glimpsed events, snippets of overheard conversation, and borrowed objects.

These days I live elsewhere and no photographic poltergeist takes my belongings. But I still feel, when I look at those things, that they lead some sort of double life and that they aren't entirely mine anymore.

Post-Modernism is a simple-sounding term, but it is also one of the least understood of the current critical labels. It is a Humpty-Dumpty word whose meaning shifts with every artist, medium and context. It is all the worse for being over-used and under-explained. The difficulty is increased by the parallels with (and apparent derivation from) the term Post-Impressionism. Whereas 'Post-Impressionism' effectively describes a style and group of artists by reference to another, 'Post-Modernism' begs more questions than it answers. What, really, is Modernism, and is it over? Is Post-Modernism a style, or a state of mind? In what sense can it be said to succeed Modernism, either temporally or ideologically?

'Modernism' is itself one of those portmanteau words whose shades of meaning and implication almost defeat definition. In everyday usage, it is so much a part of the mental furniture, such a generalised reference to a state of contemporary mind, as to escape the limits of meaning. Within the visual arts, though, it describes a set of attitudes that has dominated criticism and practice for most of the past century.

In the broadest terms, Modernism reflects a desire to 'make it new' (in the words of Ezra Pound's battlecry), to construct an art that directly reflects present conditions and experiences, without appealing for its authority to examples and images of the past. These attitudes can be found at the root of all the bewilderingly diverse 'isms' in the recent history of the visual arts. Photography itself has almost come to seem Modernist by definition, in its absolute insistence on the 'here and now' reality of whatever is in front of the camera. (This does not seem to me to be helpful. When it becomes possible to attach the label 'Modernist' to such different photographers as Edward Weston, Alexander Rodchenko, and Henri Cartier-Bresson, the term starts to conceal more fundamental disagreements than it reveals essential similarities of intention or procedure.)

The past decade has seen a fundamental shift in attitudes, and a widespread disenchantment with Modernism. This can be partly explained by the inevitable swing of the pendulum. Aesthetics and cultural theory have their 'long cycle' of shifts in basic concept as well as their more visible 'short cycles' of fashionable movements. There has been an instinctive feeling (most clearly articulated in the world of architecture, where Modernism has become associated with the style of the International Modern Movement), that Modernism is failing to deliver the goods. In a more subtle way, the very dominance and longevity of Modernism have sown the seeds of its own destruction. We now live with a 'tradition of the New', a Modernist history, and a Modernist canon which is often used as a touchstone for the authenticity of any new work — in glaring contradiction to the underlying principle of modernity.

Modernism's vulnerability to the effects of ageing and the historical process has been increased by ideas arising in the disciplines of linguistics, philosophy, anthropology and psychology. The structuralist line of thought which began with Saussure and runs through Lévi-Strauss to Barthes, Dérrida, Lacan and Foucault is now widely diffused (with varying degrees of comprehension) within the art community. The notion that images (like language) are built from a series of signs whose meaning is not fixed and absolute, but dependant on context, history, social and intellectual contract, is both familiar and widely accepted. It is only a short step from there to the making of pictures that are deliberately built from other images, and from references to familiar cultural icons. Post-Modernism proposes that, since meaning is culturally determined, to refer to the past is not to make a bogus appeal for authenticity and status, but to employ a legitimate creative procedure. Not just legitimate, indeed, but necessary and even inescapable, since our consciousness is formed not only by direct experience of life but by the imagery of the many media — advertising, film and television —which surround us with dreams of other lives. The past and its images are no longer taboo, but a source of raw material for contemporary expression.

The effect on photography has been liberating. There is a long, and long-discredited, tradition of constructed photography, which shows things not as they are but as they might be. Thankfully, it is now possible, once again, to admit to being interested in Henry Peach Robinson (though a taste for Oscar Reijlander is still problematical) and Angus McBean is enjoying a well-deserved rediscovery. The use of photography by artists to create complex, reference-filled tableaux is one of the success stories of the 1980s. In the United States, Cindy Sherman's *Untitled Film Stills* have explored issues of femininism and sex-role with appropriate style and panache. In Britain, though, Post-Modernism suffers from a reputation for difficulty, obscurity and polemic.

The publication of a substantial body of Mari Mahr's subtle and evocative photographic constructions is a doubly welcome event. Not only should it expand the audience for a photographer who is widely admired by her fellow artists, but also dispel the lingering notion that British Post-Modernist photography must necessarily be joyless and didactic.

Mahr was already a highly experienced photographer by the time the first of the works in this collection, the *Movie Pictures*, was exhibited at Open Eye in Liverpool and the Serpentine Gallery in London, in 1980. She had trained as a photographer at the School of Journalism in Budapest, and worked as a press photographer in Hungary, before coming to England in 1972 and continuing her studies at the Polytechnic of Central London (an important college for the development of photographic theory and practice in the 1970s and 1980s). Some of her earlier work in London was shown at the Photographers' Gallery in 1977 and the Riverside Studios in 1978, as well as in Holland and the United States. But the *Movie Pictures* announced a new direction. They surprised not only by their size and coherence as a series (even so short a time ago, we were unused to looking at photo works on so large a scale), but by an approach that now looks like prototypical Post-Modernism. And if references to film culture, and the use of text within the image, have now become something of a commonplace (and been left behind by Mahr), the creation of atmospheres of experience and memory, of events and feelings beyond the edge of the picture, has remained a hallmark of her work.

Where other artists have adopted film references and imagery as a lingua franca, Mari Mahr seemed to be using them for more personal and expressive purposes. In the tableau *Le Doulos* (1979), for example, the one word text *Alors* ('Then') and the title itself, are at first sight unhelpful. (*Le Doulos*, slang for 'The Informer', is not a word you will find in standard French dictionaries.) In conjunction with the image, though, they create a sense of *film noir*, of suspended action of potential threat, of seedy bedrooms and the smell of boredom mixed with caporal. Mahr does not so much 'deconstruct' the imagery, or expand on her personal experiences, as create a setting for the viewer's imagination to inhabit and develop.

Mahr has written that: 'All my images seem to come from reading books, looking at movies . . . looking at exhibitions. Although the events and situations that strike me might be quite specific, what I eventually photograph is an expression of my own reaction'.

The Chinese Woman (1982) is not only based on Maxine Hong Kingston's novel *The Woman Warrior*; the titles of the constituent pictures are straight quotations, and the images are virtually direct illustrations. But how many people will ever look at the photographs with a copy of Maxine Hong Kingston's book beside them? How does one read an image one knows to be (at least partly) illustrational, in the absence of its text? Our freedom of interpretation is opened wide, while we are made simultaneously aware of the half-hidden existence both of the photographer's intepretation of the author, and the author's interpretation of her own imaginative experience. Mari Mahr's photographs increasingly appear as palimpsests, those mediaeval manuscripts written over the more-or-less obscured remains of earlier texts. Layers of other, interwoven meanings can be sensed, without ever being quite clear.

The layering of meaning has, in the more recent works, found a direct expression in the picture-making technique. *Movie Pictures* and *The Chinese Woman* are fairly conventionally photographed tableaux. Mahr's subsequent pictures have been made via assemblages of objects set in front of background photographs. When the set is re-photographed, relationships between the two and three-dimensional are dislocated, and expectations of scale and perspective contradicted. The final picture appears to inhabit a world of its own, related to but separate from the elements from which it was created, and the world of the viewer's everyday experience.

Mari Mahr first used this technique, to great effect, in the series *Lili Brik* (1982). Lili Brik was a remarkable woman. Mathematically brilliant, trained as an artist, she became a central figure in Russian Futurist circles in the years immediately following the Revolution. Subsequently, the authorities tried to edit her out of history: independence of thought and behaviour, adherence to Futurism, and an unconventional relationship with her husband and the poet Mayakovsky (who regarded Brik as his muse and inspiration) were not the stuff from which good Socialist Realism is made. Mahr's tribute is an extended meditation, not so much an illustration as a recreation of a physical and mental atmosphere. The images avoid the icons and stylistic traits of heroic early Russian Modernism; they are built from homelier stuff — a samovar, a cup, a comfortable chair, a typewriter, a volume by Pushkin, a packet of cigarettes. Lili's love of ballet, and the room at the Brik's Moscow flat in Zhukovsky Street (where she set up a barre and took lessons from a ballerina who had danced for Diaghilev) is evoked by a row of chairs against a wall, a sheet of music and a foreground cloud of gauze like a discarded tutu.

Mari Mahr is a cosmopolitan artist; her work crosses the divide between Eastern and Western Europe, and in doing so draws on a wide range of cultural experiences. Her delight in collaging ideas and images is much closer to Continental than to British thinking; series such as *Remembering the Land* (1983) and *Virágom, Virágom* (1984) clearly refer to her Hungarian past. Ultimately, though, the strength of the pictures lies in the power of Mahr's visual imagination and its resolution in pictorial terms. I have already mentioned the peculiar spatial effects produced by

Mahr's constructional procedures. In *A Few Days in Geneva* (1985) the vertiginous dislocations of scale between the photographic backdrop of buildings and roofscapes and the overlaid foreground human elements is immediately startling, even shocking. (This is particularly so in the exhibition prints, where the human element is over life-size.) But they very soon come to seem natural, even inevitable, and assume an air of visual logic. The progression from image to image in the sequence shows a rare mastery of visual narrative.

Photographic narrative is extraordinarily difficult to pull off. Every picture has to be satisfying in itself, but also play its part in the development of the larger work. The link from picture to picture must be visually convincing, without becoming slavishly repetitious or filling in redundant detail. In *A Few Days in Geneva* picture follows picture with the rhythmic inevitability of breathing. Relationships between foreground and background are constantly, subtly varying. The foreground elements (joining man and woman with the music of Chopin's *Grande Polonaise Brillante* drifting from window to window) progress from picture to picture with unpredictable inevitability. The result is not only the most sustained of Mari Mahr's visual inventions, but the most satisfyingly 'readable' for the viewer.

Considering Mari Mahr's work as a whole, and looking for a key to its interpretation, it is not so much the writings of Roland Barthes or Victor Burgin that come to mind as Marcel Proust's great exploration of memory, experience and desire. The following passage (from *Albertine Disparue*) seems to me to be not only close to Mahr in spirit, but excellent advice on how best to approach her splendid pictures:

> The fact that our intellect is not the most subtle, the most powerful, the most appropriate instrument for grasping the truth, is only a reason the more for beginning with the intellect, and not with a subconscious intuition, a ready-made faith in presentiments. It is life that, little by little, case by case, enables us to observe that what is most important to our heart, or to our mind, is learned not by reasoning but by other powers . And then it is intellect itself which, taking note of their superiority, abdicates its sway to them upon reasoned grounds and consents to become their collaborator.

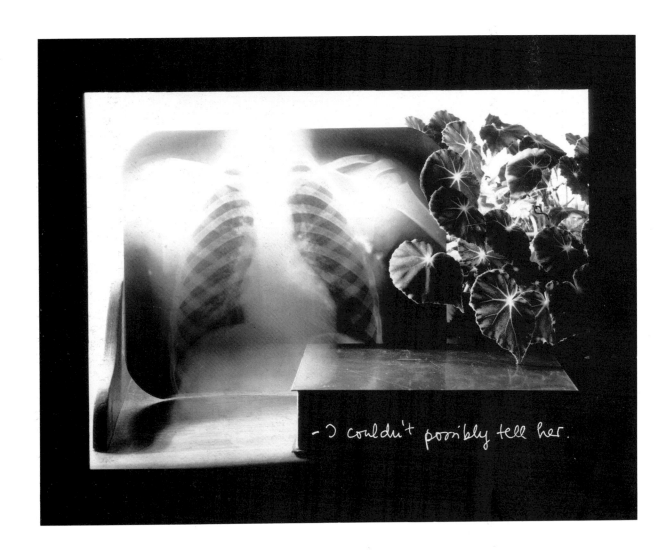

— I couldn't possibly tell her.

Some of the faces stopped to peer at us

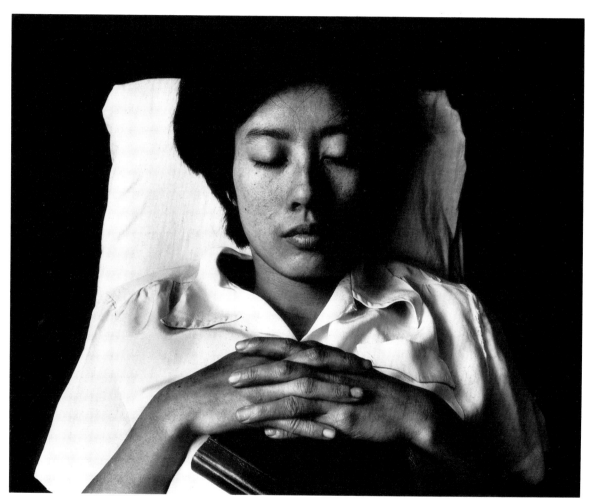

her eyes drooped and she closed her book

She could see the knife

Holding up the blanket like a little tent

She made her press crash and hiss

she shrank from his stare

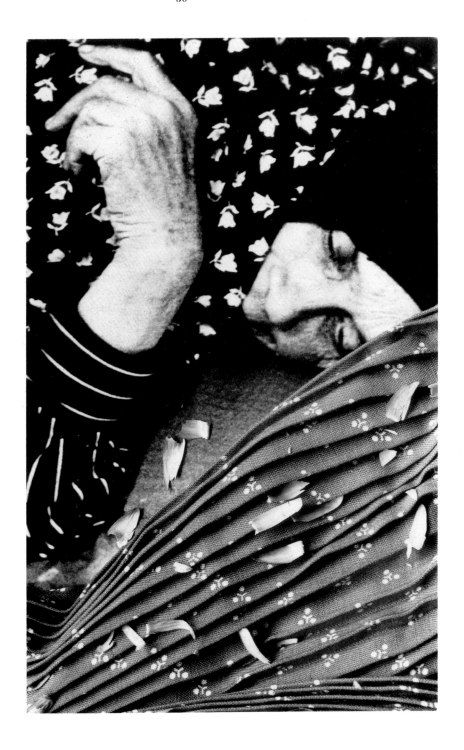

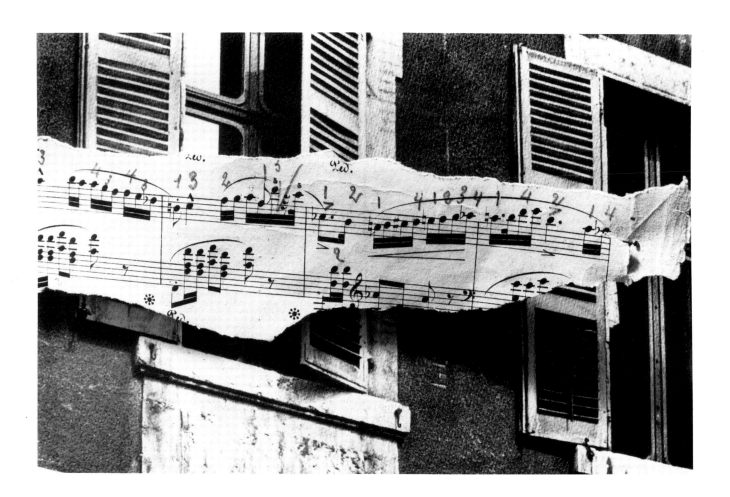

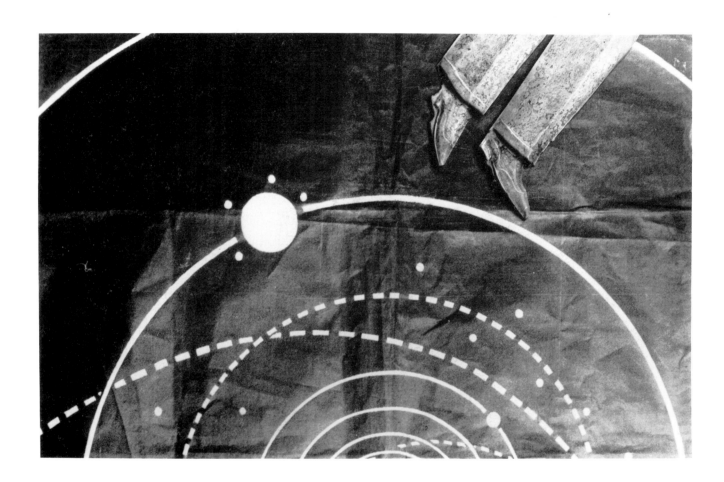